The Best of Today's
Log Homes

D0862488

Tina Skinner

Schiffer Publishing Ltd

4880 Lower Valley Road, Atglen, Pennsylvania 19310

About the Log Homes Council

This book was printed with the consent and cooperation of the members of the Log Homes Council of the National Association of Home Builders.

The Log Homes Council (LHC), part of the National Association of Home Builders, is the country's leading authority and watchdog of the log home industry. The council's mission is to educate, inspire, and advance the continued use of quality, renewable log products.

Members of the Log Homes Council include custom log home companies, handcrafters, and some of the largest manufacturers in the country. To be eligible for membership, a company must meet and maintain strict technical and ethical criteria. The Log Homes Council has enacted three important safeguards to protect consumers: mandatory log grading, the publication of a construction manual, and adherence to the council's Code of Ethics.

The Log Homes Council's website, www.loghomes.org, contains a wealth of information about the log home industry, member companies, and how to evaluate and purchase a new log home. The council further promotes its members and the industry at regional home shows, in magazines and publications, and through annual industry events. Consumers can contact the council for more information about the log home industry or LHC members by calling 800-368-5242.

Copyright © 2008 by Schiffer Publishing, Ltd.
Library of Congress Control Number: 2007942185

Designed by "Sue"
Type set in Grouch BT/Cooper Lt BT

ISBN: 978-0-7643-2954-8
Printed in China

Published by Schiffer Publishing Ltd.
4880 Lower Valley Road
Atglen, PA 19310
Phone: (610) 593-1777;
Fax: (610) 593-2002
E-mail: Info@schifferbooks.com

For the largest selection of fine reference books on this and related subjects, please visit our web site at:
www.schifferbooks.com
We are always looking for people to write books on new and related subjects. If you have an idea for a book please contact us at the above address.

Schiffer Books are available at special discounts for bulk purchases for sales promotions or premiums. Special editions, including personalized covers, corporate imprints, and excerpts can be created in large quantities for special needs. For more information contact the publisher:

This book may be purchased from the publisher.
Include $3.95 for shipping.
Please try your bookstore first.
You may write for a free catalog.

In Europe, Schiffer books are distributed by
Bushwood Books
6 Marksbury Ave.
Kew Gardens
Surrey TW9 4JF England
Phone: 44 (0) 20 8392-8585;
Fax: 44 (0) 20 8392-9876
E-mail: info@bushwoodbooks.co.uk
Website: www.bushwoodbooks.co.uk
Free postage in the U.K., Europe;
air mail at cost.

Contents

Introduction 5
Houses 6
  Feeling Connected...........6
  Winter Wonderland.......14
  Being Together 18
  Place in History 22
  Lady of the Lake 28
  Family Fun 32
  Golden Glory................40
  A Lot in a Little 44

Cypress So Sweet...........50
Southern Charm 56
Rural Retreat 62
Woodland Hideaway.....68
The New Homestead.....72
Porch Light....................78
Lofty Ideas.....................84
Extended Family 88
Family Frontier.............92
Overlooking the Lake....96

Outward Bound...........104
It's a Wrap....................108
Aqua Gem....................114
Familial Embrace........116
Packing It In 122
Suite Deal....................124
Lake Luster 130
Separate but Equal 134
All Decked Out 138
Contributors 144

Introduction

By The Log Home Council

The first homes built in colonial America were log homes. For many years, homes built with solid log walls were the only type of home constructed in this country. They were simple, primitive structures, but their prevalence earned the log home a special place in American lore, right next to baseball and apple pie. Somewhere along the way, though, the log home gave way to wood-frame, brick, or stone homes. By the middle of the 20th century, log homes were considered little more than a relic leftover from a simpler time. But that sentiment has changed.

Today, the log home has made its comeback. Attracted by a combination of historic craftsmanship and modern construction technologies, more people than ever are choosing log homes. Renowned for their inherent beauty, sustainability, and energy-efficiency, log homes are undeniably tranquil. The log home, once relegated to lakefronts and mountainsides, now blends seamlessly into traditional suburban and even urban environments.

The resurgence of log homes is likely what drew you to this book. Log homes are the most beautiful and artistic type of homes, but they are also complicated to research and build. Even if you purchased a new or custom home in the past, you may feel overwhelmed by the considerations necessary when building a log home. More than any other type of home, a new log home offers you numerous choices and ways to personalize your design. You can choose to customize your floor plan, wood species, log profile style, fastening system, and many other facets of your new home. Such diverse options can be overwhelming to a new log homebuyer, but The Best of Today's Log Homes makes researching and understanding these homes easier.

Each of the companies featured in this book are members of the Log Homes Council, the country's foremost technical and ethical log home organization. All LHC members, including the 28 whose homes are showcased in this book, must meet strict technical criteria when planning and engineering their homes. That safeguard leaves you able to choose virtually any options for your new log home with the assurance that your home will be technically sound, meet local building codes, and last for generations to come.

Modern log homes may bear a stylish resemblance to their colonial forbearers, but – inside and out – they are a far cry from those primitive dwellings. Once held together by handcrafted corner systems or even mud, today's log homes can be engineered to withstand tornadoes and hurricane-force winds. And all types of amenities, including luxurious master suites, wireless media rooms, and restaurant-quality kitchens can be built into your dream home. Don't let the log home's rustic appearance fool you – today's log home is ready for the 21st century.

A log home also makes it easy to be green. Homes with solid log walls are the only types of homes built with renewable natural resources. As a log homeowner, you will live in a house that is energy-efficient and sustainable. If environmental impact and a decreased carbon footprint are a priority, you can choose a log home manufacturer that uses only standing-dead timber in their home packages. Other manufacturers harvest from sustainable forests or pledge to plant as many trees as they cut.

Because of the naturally-occurring heating and cooling properties of solid log walls, your home will use less energy than a wood-frame home of comparable size. Building a log home is the environmentally friendly decision, but the extra money you will save on electricity is a nice benefit, too.

The homes and the companies you will see in this book are some of the finest in the country. By choosing to build a log home, you will be following a tradition started centuries ago by some of this country's first settlers. But the home you choose to build – no matter what size, what style, or wood species – will be modern, stylish, and built to your exact specification.

The journey to build a new log home is not a solitary effort. You may work with architects, engineers, manufacturers, designers, and builders during the construction process. As you begin thinking about a new log home, remember the styles, amenities, and manufacturers on the pages that follow. Using this book as a guide and the log home companies that follow as a resource, you will build one of today's best log homes.

Feeling Connected

Photography by Roger Wade
Manufactured by Barna Log Homes
Built by Phil and Nancy Lavely
Designed by Phil and Nancy Lavely

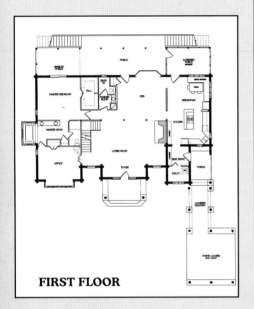

FIRST FLOOR

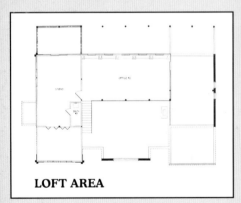

LOFT AREA

BASEMENT

A covered colonnade connects the home to sheltered parking area, easing the transition from car to side entryway. The front entryway is attractively sheltered beneath a two-tiered portico, and a huge expanse of back porch, offering this family lots of opportunities to get outside and enjoy their secluded woodland atmosphere. Like the logs that unify the exterior elements, the inside of the home has been finished throughout in full logs, as well as plank floors and wood paneled ceilings, making the indoors feel at one with the out. Most of the living in this home takes place on the first floor, where the master suite opens off a den and living room area, and connects via the bath with a private office. However, a large, walkout basement area is a getaway within the home, with a big media room for sporting events and special screenings. There's a guest bedroom and full bath downstairs, as well as a powder room and extensive storage. In the loft area, a half bath serves a big office and studio, destinations for creativity as well as the wonderful view.

A covered walkway connects the parking area with a side entrance. It's a destination unto itself, but also a blessed aid on a rainy day, when there are groceries to transport from the car to the nearby kitchen.

An attractive portico and matching porte-cochere greet guests on arrival to this attractive woodland home. Character logs flank the front porch, and attest to the unique nature of the home, as does the light-finish on the logs.

The great room extends back into a family room area, warmed by a fireplace within a soaring stonewall.

The front entryway leads right into the great room of the home, an impressive introduction located under a loft office.

There are a number of seating options in this house, from barstools next to the kitchen island counter, to a sunny breakfast nook in the kitchen, to a nice table nestled next to a bay window in the great room.

Dining also extends outside to an extensive porch, screened-in porch, and deck area located along the rear side of the house.

A specious guest bedroom in the basement has a nice window to feed sunlight in.

Like the rest of the home, the master bed and bath carry on the log-home theme, with the exception of a couple of painted walls that add color to the textural wood surrounds. A cathedral ceiling overlooks the bedroom, and windows open the view through the gabled porch beyond.

Winter Wonderland

Photography by Rich Frutchey
Manufactured by
Alta Log Homes
Built by Alta Log Homes
of Greene County
Designed by Andrew and Elizabeth
Lloyd and Alta Log Homes
of Greene County

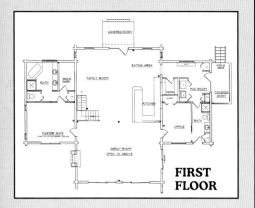

FIRST FLOOR

SECOND FLOOR

This ski-lodge/second home looks deceptively small from its driveway elevation. Inside there's a lot of living space. A central area includes a great room, family room, dining area and kitchen, all open and overlooked by a loft. The master bedroom suite enjoys its own wing of the house, as does a home office/mud and laundry room. Two bedrooms upstairs are perfect for guests or storage. Architecturally, the home was handily engineered with a standard central nave, left open on the rear side to create a wall of glass windows. To compliment the mountain views, dormers crown the front of the home's central portion, extending the upstairs and creating two spacious upstairs bedrooms. Two side wings contribute the cozier portions of the home under a single story room. Two covered entryways help the homeowners gain clean access in a climate that's not always clement.

Bump-out extensions on either side of a central core, as well as extended dormers over the central roofline, create a sense that an historic log cabin has been expanded with a growing family. The inside tells a different story, with rising cathedral ceilings and open spaces snugly insulated from the cold elements. Built to the highest energy efficient standards, and awarded the Energy Star rating.

A snug little family room sits off the main entrance to the home, acting as a greeting area for guests.

A great room at the back of the home becomes the natural gathering place, next to a grand view and nestled under a majestic cathedral ceiling. A massive stone chimney is perfect for hanging the stockings by the fire.

A loft area overlooks the great room. Two bedrooms and a bath are upstairs, their floors forming a lowered ceiling for the kitchen, dining, and family room areas.

An open kitchen and dining area connect with the mudroom and laundry areas. A pantry around the corner is conveniently located near a covered entry to the home.

The master bedroom and bath suite is just that – sweet. Plenty of room has been afforded the homeowners under a cathedral ceiling, and a whirlpool tub offers a wonderful way to relax after a day on the slopes.

Being Together

Photography by Kim Prochazka
Manufactured by Beaver Mountain Log and Cedar Homes
Built by Arrow Brook Building & Remodel

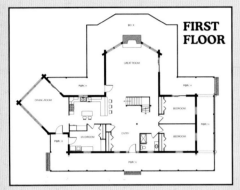

FIRST FLOOR

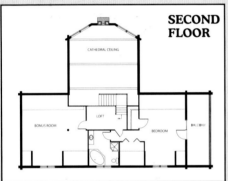

SECOND FLOOR

A wrap-around porch and three handsome dormers add to the home's classic appeal, welcoming guests to come in and stay awhile.

This log home is designed to bring family together. The kitchen serves as the central hub, connecting the great room to the dining area that is surrounded by glass walls to allow everyone to enjoy the view while dining. A wrap around porch and deck space outside provide plenty of room for entertaining. A laundry room/mudroom conveniently lies to one side of the house while two bedrooms lie on the opposite side. Upstairs, the large master suite allows for quiet moments of escape. An adaptable bonus room is perfect for guests or as a recreation room. Family space is maximized in this classic log home retreat.

Photographs adorn the entryway as a tribute to the homeowner's son, a NYC firefighter who passed away in service on September 11, 2001.

A love of the outdoors is reflected in the great room's rustic décor while the grand fireplace is accented by their son's various trophies on and above the mantel.

Opposite page:
The large professional kitchen is
every cook's delight. Its central loca-
tion and countertop seating add to
its usefulness, while plenty of natural
light adds charm.

Left:
A cathedral ceiling crowns the
home's dining room, where walls
of windows capture the glory of the
secluded view.

A private balcony opens off the
master suite, tucked beneath the
eaves of the roof.

Place in History

Photography by Judy Lawrence
Manufactured by Custom Log Homes
Built by Hathorn Construction
Designed by Richard Dooley

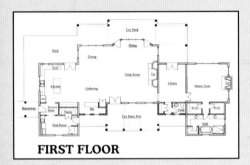

FIRST FLOOR

The wrap around porch framed with natural logs provides an interesting welcome and "historic" feel to this mountaintop estate. The liberal use of indigenous rock, stacked in a ledgelay fashion also evokes the house-building craftsmanship of times past.

Located in a sea of aspen, the hand hewn, chinked logs, the stonework, and the cedar shake roof contribute to a sense that this is a log homestead meticulously crafted years ago by early settlers. This was not by accident, as the massive wall logs with handcrafted dovetail corners and a timber truss roof system were carefully antiqued to perfect the illusion. In contrast, the modern floor plan with seamless transitions between the various gathering areas, kitchen and great room allows the owners to entertain even the most discriminating guest. A breezeway connects the home to the garage at one end of the home while the master suite enjoys its' own secluded entry via the library.

The variegated patina of the hewn wall logs gives a warm and ageless appearance, and the traditional timber trusses support a raftered roof system with grey washed decking.

An eat-in kitchen combines a table with the central island. Kitchen windows overlook the covered walkway from garage to the kitchen's service entry. The antique finish on the bead board cabinetry and the hand-troweled plaster and ceramic tiles blend to timeless perfection; elegant but not pretentious.

Above left:
A dining area is positioned in a windowed corner under the cathedral ceiling crowning the great room area.

Above right and below:
The master suite enjoys its own cozy fireplace, under the inspiring space of a cathedral ceiling. Red curtains unify the room, while offering privacy in a room blessed with two walls of windows.

The master bath is accessed through a hallway, passing his and hers walk-in closets. Like the rest of the home, the beauty and individual character of each log is defined by the chinking.

Lady of the Lake

Photography by Rich Frutchey
Manufactured by
Estemerwalt Log Homes

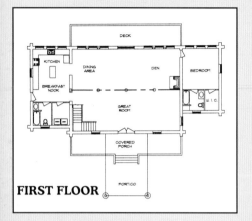

FIRST FLOOR

SECOND FLOOR

A log home presents an elegant greeting to returning family and friends who flock to this lakeside retreat.

Cabin is too simplified a word for this small, lakefront home. Elegant rooflines set this log structure apart, and inside the space has been kept breathtakingly open in honor of the atmosphere. A love of log is evident in the full round posts, and full round log, both outside and throughout the interior décor. Four small bedrooms help parcel out the population as groups of friends and families make their pilgrimages to this gloriously isolated little retreat.

A post-and-rail type balustrade frames the view from this deck overlooking the lake.

A fireplace warms the den area, part and parcel of a den and great room gathering place.

Opposite page:
The kitchen, off in its own nook on the first floor, connects the cook to the lake, and offers a breakfast nook that tends to be a gathering place long after the dishes have been cleared.

The dining area is flanked by stairs to the second floor.

The master bedroom is tucked into a wing off the main house with its own private view of the lakefront.

Family Fun

Photography by Roger Wade Studios
Manufactured by Expedition
Log Homes, LLC
Built by Cabin Fever Construction, LLC
Designed by Expedition Log Homes

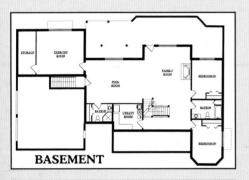

BASEMENT

FIRST FLOOR

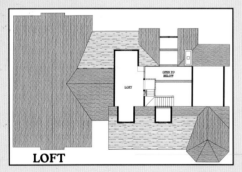

LOFT

This wonderful home has it all for a busy family. The kids have a downstairs to die for, their bedrooms opening into a large family room area and poolroom. Upstairs, the parents have their master suite on the other side of the house, isolated for glorious privacy at the rear of the home. Activity was uppermost in the planning of this spacious home. Besides the poolroom, there's an exercise room and lots of family areas to congregate and socialize, like a sunroom, a great room, and an expansive back deck and porches front and back, and even a loft area overlooking the great room. The kitchen sits at the hub of all the activity, accessed easily via the garage and the spacious foyer.

A wonderful log home greets guests to this busy family home. Beyond the beautiful façade, this home has been designed for lots of fun, with big rooms, and lots of them, for family activities and entertaining.

A pretty porch greets the many guests that come to enjoy the company of outgoing parents and their children. The promise of rich log home architecture evidenced on the porch is carried throughout the homc.

Like the interior, the exterior is all about recreation. An expansive deck spills down into a rambling patio and the great stretch of lawn beyond.

A stairwell defined by character logs and a rustic rail greets visitors as they enter the home.

A great room is the focal gathering place in this home, warmed by a fireplace and overlooked by a custom window that fills a full wall from floor to cathedral ceiling. A loft provides a unique vantage point, and acts as a magnet for children.

A window seat provides a private nook in the loft area, a wonderful place to escape and hide away, and an inevitable draw for children.

An office occupies a multi-faceted extension in the front of the home, providing a watchtower vantage over the entryway of the home.

The kitchen and dining room are connected and open under the wood beams supporting the second-story loft. Cabinetry was selected to match the exposed logs inside, unifying the look.

A sunroom occupies a back corner
of the home, with two walls of doors
and windows to illuminate the space
and open the view.

The master suite occupies a wonderful, private wing behind the garage and separated from the main house by a utility room. As the homeowners downsize, it might easily be converted to an apartment for an in-law or tenant.

Golden Glory

Manufactured by Gastineau Log Homes, Inc.

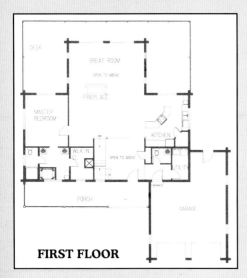

FIRST FLOOR

SECOND FLOOR

A porte-cochere provides a sheltered entrance at the front of this expansive log home, while a long porch welcomes visitors to the front door.

The back of the home is flanked by an extensive deck, and shines in the glory of a custom eave wall of windows. Quarter-round windows form a petal-like ring atop fixed picture windows and sliding glass doors.

Oak creates a golden glow for the logs that clad this spacious rural retreat. Though seemingly modest from the front, the backside of this home attests to the outdoor nature of the homeowners. A wall of windowpane connects indoors with out, and a broad deck encircles the back of the home. A central fireplace offers warmth throughout the rooms that surround it, the stone chimney rising up through the large loft area to share that heat with two guest rooms on the second floor.

The entryway introduces first-time visitors to the spacious expanse that characterizes the interior of the home.

The kitchen area has its own nook off the great room area, overlooked by a great-beamed ceiling.

Various angles show how the home revolves around the central fireplace, with lots of opportunities to congregate and interact.

A beamed ceiling overlooks the master bedroom, finished in drywall. The rusticity of log home sensibility is carried into the bath, where a stone surround nests a spacious whirlpool tub.

A Lot in a Little

Photography by Roger Wade
Manufactured by
Golden Eagle Log Homes
Designed by Golden Eagle Log Homes

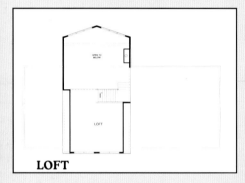

LOFT

FIRST FLOOR

A planter in the entry court of this little log home tells newcomers two things: he likes to fish, she loves to garden. Every inch of their home and yard reflects who they are, and what they love.

A covered porch with a screened door offers old-fashioned welcome.

Your first glance at this floor plan might convince you there's not much to this house. However, the floor plans don't reveal the walkout basement, and the images reveal that these homeowners know how to pack a lot of fun into a little space. They've moved their focus outward, too, with a backyard campsite complete with fire pit. There's always room in the loft for overnight visitors, or they can stay in the log lean-to created for friends and family who love the outdoors.

A prow-faced rear extension rises above a walkout basement, garnished with a deck. The deck railing is finished with black wrought iron to help preserve the view over a lovingly tended garden.

Decking on the rear of the house offers dining al fresco, and satisfies the homeowner's frequent yearning for fresh air.

Camp has been made in the back yard, with a fire pit as its central jewel.

A great room focuses on a wall of windows and is the favorite place within the small home.

The kitchen and dining area are connected to the great room. One side of the kitchen is flanked by a wall and cabinctry that forms the foyer area. The dining table cozies up to a finished log wall next to the French doors that open to the master bedroom.

A rose glow reflects the feminine touch in the master suite.

The loft offers a sunny escape area high above life's little concerns.

It's all fun and games in the basement area, where a home bar and musical entertainment are main attractions amidst beloved collectibles.

Cypress So Sweet

*Photography by Steven McBride
Photography
Manufactured by Hearthstone, Inc.
Built by Troy Osbourne
Designed by Architect David Sellers*

FIRST FLOOR

SECOND FLOOR

A simple gravel drive approaches this rustic masterpiece, with a porte-cochere ready for parking. The log home was created with rough-hewn logs and chinking for an authentic, historic appeal.

An alcove off the main house appears to be supported by the great fieldstone fireplace and rock wall surrounding a patio area. A detail shot reveals the feathered edge siding created from cypress harvested nearby.

From a distance you've no idea what awaits. Close-up, this lodge is rich in details. People who've visited the lodge proclaim that these images don't begin to do it justice. Nonetheless these are great images and you'll want to spend time absorbing some of the incredible details. This lodge sits on a private, 1,000-plus acre estate near Charleston, South Carolina. The naturally shaped support posts, feathered edge siding and trim were harvested on site from the owner's cypress groves. The wall logs were crafted from Eastern White Pine in east Tennessee. The naturally shaped floor joists were selectively cut from Eastern Hemlock in Vermont, after the sap had run so the bark would have a better chance to stay attached to the timber.

Finished tree trunks support the front entryway, and cross-sectional logs were hand-fashioned for this artful door, set amidst dovetailed log construction.

A detail shot reveals the post and beam craftsmanship that supports the porch roof.

Another shot reveals details of the front porch.

Bearskins and a stained glass window framed in cypress greet visitors upon entry.

Leather furniture cozies up comfortably to the great room fireplace. There's a forest feeling to this great room, with actual trees rising up to support the roof. A custom chandelier fashioned from a canoe illuminates the dining area, while hunting scenes adorn enormous tapestries hung on the far wall.

A view from the rafters offers a sense of scale across the great room.

The bark was left on the edges of the floor joists, while an unfinished young tree and cypress knees finish a corner in this home office.

A nook houses a collection of hunting gear, framed by post and beam.

Handcrafted molding frames the door and window in this breakfast nook.

One inch thick hand-hewn log veneer used on interior non-structural walls for effect.

True to the rustic roots of the log cabin, the commode takes its clues from our forefathers, while keeping it up to contemporary standards.

Southern Charm

Photography by
Charles Brooks Photography
Manufactured by Heritage Log Homes
Designed by Tim & Connie Wilson

FIRST FLOOR

SECOND FLOOR

This pretty belle fits in with the landscape, exuding southern charm and grace amidst an immaculate green lawn.

You have to get close-up to this home to realize it's log construction. From a distance, it's form and color simply speaks southern plantation style. Up close, though, it is imbued with all the richness and heritage of a chinked log home. Built shotgun style on a big scale, the home feeds off a central passageway of foyer and great room stretching the length between front and back doors. A cupola crowns the home, and wide verandas provide the skirt to this southern belle, complete with graceful porch columns and a wealth of white balustrades.

A front veranda takes advantage of a lakefront view and the cooling breezes off the water. A balcony above offers the same amenity to the second floor.

A screened porch stretches the length of one side of the house, with a lake view for the occupants, along with bug-free dining.

Catwalk and loft areas overlook the expansive family area on the first floor.

The great room and dining area are interconnected amidst this airy environment framed in white log.

Milk and cream tones characterize this classic kitchen, nestled next to the great room.

Guest bedrooms upstairs were designed to welcome. Each enjoys its own bath, and opens to the second floor balcony overlooking the lake. White rafters and soaring ceiling add to the enticement.

The master suite enjoys its own view of the lake, commanding an entire side of the house that features a master bath and walk-in closet of enviable proportions.

Rural Retreat

Photography by James Ray Spahn
Manufactured by Hiawatha Log Homes
Built by Tom Hall Contracting
Designed by Homeowner: Barbara Piper
& Hiawatha Log Homes

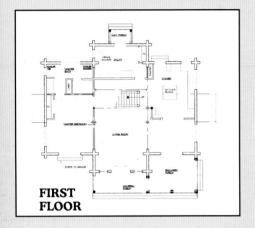

FIRST FLOOR

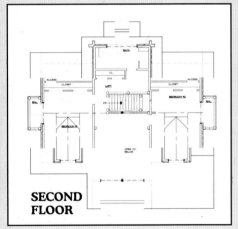

SECOND FLOOR

A steep roof caps the portico entrance to this charming little cabin in the woods with a full-length front porch.

At the end of a dirt road in the wilderness, this lovely cabin awaits the next return of loving owners. Someday they hope to retire to this 1,304 square-foot paradise. In the meantime, three bedrooms provide refuge for friends and family, along with lots of areas to gather. Dormer windows feed the small upstairs with sunlight, and a small balcony serves up a tall retreat. Hidden in back are a screened-in porch and a covered porch, too.

A fieldstone fireplace warms the great room, where a two-story glass wall gives a glimpse into the wild world beyond.

A kitchen island was constructed with matching logs, in keeping with the walls and a beamed ceiling. Likewise custom designed Birdseye maple cabinetry, a plate rack, and a butcher-block counter are in matching pine, all created by a local cabinet maker.

Opposite page:
A dining nook opens via French doors to an enclosed porch beyond.

Sliding glass doors ensure that an enclosed porch is useful year round.

A master bedroom opens via-French doors to the backyard. The master bath features a whirlpool corner tub with a view.

Both bedrooms upstairs feature dormer windows as well as double doors that open onto small balconies.

Woodland Hideaway

Photography and Styling by Franklin and Esther Schmidt
Manufactured by Hilltop Log & Timber Homes
Built by Hilltop Log & Timber Homes and Bandit Builders
Designed by Hilltop Log & Timber Homes

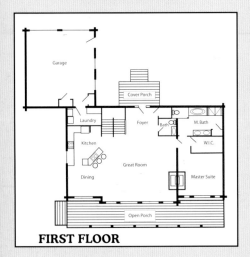

FIRST FLOOR

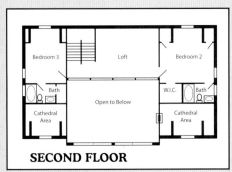

SECOND FLOOR

A portico mirrors the triangle of windows above, creating a doubly impressive entry to this 2,710 square-foot log home getaway. Gravel landscaping keeps maintenance to a minimum.

A log home in the woods provides a great getaway, and a dreamed of retirement plan for a small family. This second home has spacious downstairs living, along with a big master suite, and two bedrooms upstairs that enjoy their own baths on opposite sides of a shared, open loft. The pretty blue roofline makes way for cathedral ceilings above the master bedroom and the dining areas at the back of the home, as well as a huge central great room.

A backyard image exposes this woodland roost, with a walkout basement, elevated deck and great room enjoying the view at a bird's-eye level.

An entry foyer feeds visitors into the main areas of the home under an overhanging loft.

Opposite page:
The great room features walls of stone and wood, adding to the effect of rustic retreat.

Left:
Cabinetry was chosen to match the log finish on the interior of the home.

Left:
A dining area opens to the deck, illuminated by stained glass lighting fixtures suspended from a support beam.

Right:
A fireplace warms the master suite, which extends the full length of one side of the home.

The New Homestead

*Photography by Fred Hansen
and Roger Wade
Manufactured by
Hochstetler Milling, Ltd.
Designed by Hochstetler Milling, Ltd.*

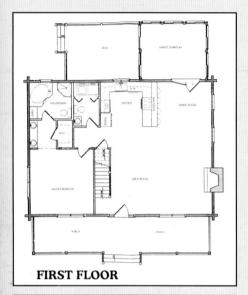

FIRST FLOOR

SECOND FLOOR

Front dormers and a house-length porch are part and parcel of the country charm exuded by this log home. A stone chimney climbs an exterior wall. From the front, you wouldn't know that the fireplace warms a room full of windows, adding contemporary luxury to the living areas in the back of the home while more traditional, small windows overlook the front.

A sweet 2,041 square-foot log home exudes traditional cabin charm. Though only a 40-foot stretch across the front, the home has been carefully organized to make sure that the family members enjoy privacy, along with a generous allowance of open, shared space. Two bedrooms are tucked upstairs next to a loft and a shared bath for the children. A dormer in front feeds the front bedroom with light, while a shed dormer extends the roofline in back. Downstairs, the master suite was designed to include a walk-in closet and dressing area, as well as a bath suite outfitted with shower, whirlpool tub, and storage space. Besides a big great room, open to the kitchen and dining area, a gabled sunroom and deck allow family members to move out toward a wonderful, rural view.

The family great room nestles under a cathedral ceiling, overlooked by a loft area. Open access to the second story is a great way for family members to communicate back and forth.

The kitchen is open on two sides, allowing the cook to feel she's part of the action when preparing meals.

Top:
The informal dining area is connected to the kitchen via a peninsula, and to sunroom and deck beyond for al fresco dining.

Above and left:
Gable windows cap walls of glass in the sunroom extension. For privacy, shades drop neatly down to envelope this space after dark.

The master bath suite on the first floor has tongue-and-groove paneling throughout, as well as amenities like a whirlpool tub and great views from every window.

Two bedrooms share a full bath upstairs. The front bedroom, shown, utilizes a dormer to expand its space and natural lighting, as well as storage space under the sloping roof.

Porch Light

Photography by Roger Wade Studio, Inc.
Manufactured by Honest Abe
Log Homes, Inc.
Built by Volunteer Log Homes
Designed by Honest Abe
Log Homes, Inc.

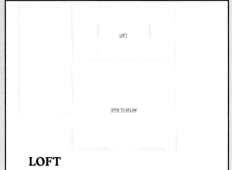

FIRST FLOOR

LOFT

Porches wrap more than three-quarters of this home, and what they don't have surrounded, a deck has covered. Set in the midst of an expansive meadow, these homeowners are blissfully prepared to enjoy it from every angle. The home is positioned for ground floor living, with three bedrooms encircling a great open living area. The cathedral ceiling that overlooks the great room provides space for a small loft, where family members can find solitude or inspiration. And though the home is impressive in appearance and layout, it is in no way pretentious. There is no formal entryway. The front door opens right into a dining room, and with this kind of privacy, the family feels as comfortable dining out on the front porch as the back. Six doors open from inside to out, with each of the three bedrooms enjoying their own access to outside and fresh air via passage through a covered porch.

A wealth of covered porch characterizes this remote log home. The steep rooflines are to create ceiling space and light for the rooms within, as the living takes place primarily on the expansive first floor.

All welcome and no formality, a front porch provides a lot of outdoor living space. The front door opens to a dining area off the kitchen.

A rear elevation emphasizes the remote character of this log home. The wall of window and chimney that backs the great room is the only side of the house not shielded in covered porch, but instead rises above decking.

Conscious of their rural heritage, the homeowners decorated with country in mind.

Wide screen entertainment caps a huge fireplace, flanked by walls of window in this great room. Exposed beams elevate the room to airy heights, overlooked by a small loft at the top of a spiral staircase.

Kitchen and dining areas share space with the living area, all in one great room.

The master suite commands one whole side of the house, with views from both bed and bath.

Below, left:
Visitors can bunk in the loft. It's also a great place to daydream.

Below:
Each bedroom offers a route directly to the outdoors for this family of nature lovers.

Lofty Ideals

*Photography by John Hamel
Manufactured by
Kuhns Bros. Log Homes, Inc.
General Contracting by
S&M Contractors
Designed by Kuhns Bros.
Log Homes, Inc.*

FIRST FLOOR

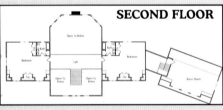

SECOND FLOOR

A broad circular driveway is as grand as the portico that greets visitors. Beyond, they enter a sweep of great hallway that is nothing short of awe-inspiring.

An incredible great room greets visitors to this home, and provides a wealth of space where the family can play in the center of the home. A doublewide stairwell leads from the foyer to the broad catwalk that crosses the cavernous grand central room and connects bedrooms on either side of the house. More intimate spaces, albeit still generously proportioned, are found in the two side wings. The master suite commands a whole wing for itself, while another plays host to kitchen and office, and connects via mudroom to the three-bay garage.

A broad staircase is one of the first sites to greet visitors, ascending to a catwalk loft that traverses the great central room.

Living room and dining area share space within the incredible great room. Walls of windows flank a stone chimney, and rich timbers outline the expanse of roofline.

A kitchen serves the great room next door, set up like a great buffet for entertaining.

A home office opens off of the kitchen, with a wall of windows offering advantageous views of the driveway.

The master suite opens to a back porch, and enjoys its own wing of the property, isolated from the main house by a walk-in-closet and bath that act as sound barriers.

Two spacious bedrooms enjoy the upstairs area, each to its own side, with the rafters exposed to add height and interest to the architecture.

Extended Family

Photography by Elvie Miller
Manufactured by
Meadowlark Log Homes
Reassembled by Miller Pinecraft
Designed by Don Jordan
Design and Drafting

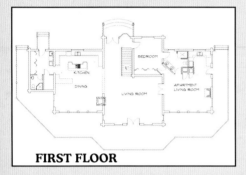

FIRST FLOOR

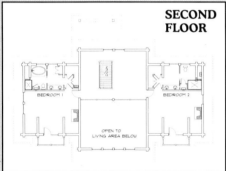

SECOND FLOOR

An expansive home was designed to accommodate two families comfortably under one roof.

Burgundy roofing crowns an expanse of home and matching garage in a spread built to house two families. An in-law suite is interconnected with the family's living areas on the first floor, so aging parents can take part in the central household, and everyone can enjoy space of their own. The main house includes living areas on the first floor, and two bedrooms' upstairs, including the master suite on the opposite side of the home as the in-laws. Large exterior decks envelope and unites the house, designed with family harmony uppermost in mind.

An expansive exterior deck wraps the back of the home, while covered porches shelter the front and sides. For a family interested in the outdoors, this home affords them ample opportunity to move their household activities into the fresh air.

River stone fronts a great chimney and fireplace in the living room area, the focal point of two homes in one.

A bear overlooks the double doors that open between the separate apartment and the great room.

Opposite page:
The kitchen and dining room in the main house open through a long archway cut through logs that form a wall between them and the great room. River stone that matches the fireplace forms the kitchen island, with an extended countertop for dining.

A loft area provides additional living space, and connects two secluded upstairs bedrooms on either side of the house.

The in-law suite has its own gas-log fireplace and lots of windows to make it a bright, cheerful place.

Family Frontier

Photography by Roger Wade
Manufactured by
Meadow Valley Log Homes
Built by Meadow Valley Log Homes
& Meiner's Lumber
Designed by Bonnie and Don Robley,
Meadow Valley Log Homes

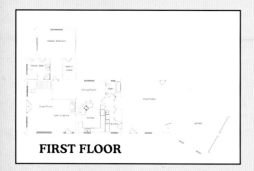

FIRST FLOOR

SECOND FLOOR

Snowbound is just what this family likes to be in their remote mountain home. A front porch is welcoming, and it's always warm and dry inside.

A family of four fits comfortably in this chalet style log home. There's lots of great open space where they get together downstairs, including a hobby room on the first floor where snow skis, snowmobiles, and other outdoor recreation gear is stored. A guest room upstairs welcomes friends and family who come to share in the fun with this outdoors loving brood.

A great room is the focal point of the home, with a big fireplace and lots of window glass to soak in the view. Trophies attest to the homeowner's love of hunting and other sports.

A three-sided island in the kitchen provides lots of workspace, as well as an attractive spot for family members to dine. A larger dining area just beyond takes advantage of a beautiful window view.

A small open loft provides a view over the living room, and serves as a central meeting point for the three upstairs bedrooms.

A family room in the basement enjoys its own fireplace, and is a favorite hangout for the young members of the family.

A master suite on the first floor is set apart in a private wing in the back of the home.

Three bedrooms upstairs are finished in log and house the children and many guests who come to enjoy the abundance of outdoor sports to be found locally.

Overlooking the Lake

Photography by Jim Battles
Manufactured by
Northeastern Log Homes
Built by Jim Naville
Designed by Ned and Sue Pfau

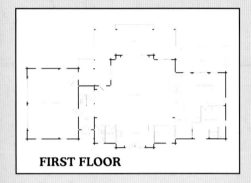

FIRST FLOOR

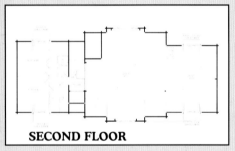

SECOND FLOOR

Exposed beams support an extended roofline, creating shelter for the rear deck and expanding the opportunities to be outside enjoying the view of the lake.

This home was carefully planned to take advantage of beautiful lake views from nearly every room. The living room, master bedroom, and one upstairs room are oriented toward the precious view, and timber framing keeps the space open to allow for large windows and unobstructed views. Rich detailing inside and out attest to the care the homeowners took in planning their lakeside retreat.

Log siding details a dormer, a nice touch in keeping with the rest of the home.

A front entryway is beautifully framed in log, an extension of the care taken in designing this log home, inside and out.

A beautiful fireplace creates an intimate focus under the soaring roof of the great room.

A fitting chandelier illuminates the entryway staircase.

Far Right and opposite page: Two dining areas enjoy positions within the great room. A round table is handy both for meals and for fun and games in the evenings and on rainy days.

A handsome kitchen enjoys its own space under the cathedral roof at the front of the home. A pantry and laundry room sits just around the corner.

Al fresco dining on a deck overlooking the lake is the highlight of weekend getaways. The same handsome timber framing inside extends out, supporting an extended roofline that shelters the deck.

A master bedroom suite is palatial in size, and exquisite in detail. A fireplace warms the bedroom, and great rafters frame a cathedral roof.

Two guest bedrooms tucked under the eaves share the upstairs and a bath.

Outward Bound

*Photography by
Roger Wade Photography
Manufactured by Precision Craft Log
& Timber Homes
Built by Everest Construction
Designed by Mountain Architects, Inc.*

FIRST FLOOR

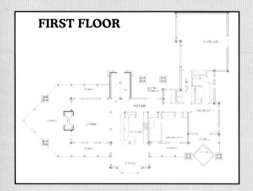

SECOND FLOOR

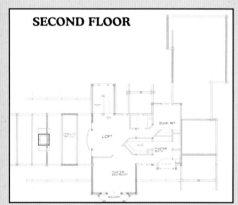

Extended roofline on the back of the house enables lots of outdoors living. A double-sided fireplace, and a hot tub, makes it possible to be outside, even in the worst of weather.

**Opposite page:
The great room is overlooked by a wonderful cathedral ceiling, outlined with hand-hewn beams. A flagstone chimney climbs one wall, adding emphasis to the room's height. The mounted buck on the wall over the fireplace is evidence of Don Robley's hobby of taxidermy. Since these photographs were taken, he has built a taxidermy shop using Meadow Valley log siding.**

It's obvious that the outdoors was uppermost in mind when this wonderful wilderness hybrid milled log and timber frame home was designed. The prow-shaped porch enjoys a big fireplace to extend its usefulness into colder months, and a porch off the bedroom was custom designed to incorporate a hot tub.

The interior finishes of this home add the elegance of a modern lifestyle while not detracting from the mountain theme of wood and stone. Earth tones are common on walls and fabrics. It's very civilized living, with a great room for gathering and plenty of guest rooms for visitors, featuring leather furniture with hints of color coming from accent pieces. The master bedroom has a private balcony, too.

Interesting to know, the family is very proud that they have only five sheets of drywall in the entire home. Since they love the natural look of logs and wood, this is what they used!

A work island doubles as bar seating, and under counter storage. This half-wall keeps the view open through the great room area.

A bump out provides a great gathering place for card games, camaraderie, and, of course, dining.

A master suite on the second floor is inspiring in both architecture and appointments.

It's a Wrap

Photography by Rich Frutchey
Manufactured by Real Log Homes
Built by C. M. Allaire & Sons, Inc.
Designed by C. M. Allaire & Sons, Inc.

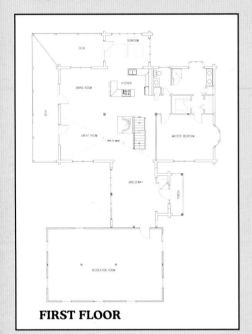

FIRST FLOOR

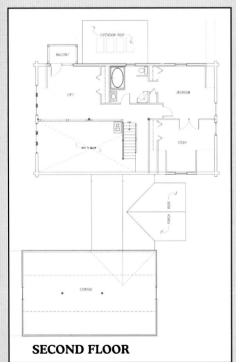

SECOND FLOOR

Even the front approach has a sheltered feel, with a welcoming covered entryway.

The welcoming, vaulted entry area opens into a grand, cathedral-style great room featuring exposed log roof rafters, patio doors, and step-up windows. The breezeway doubles as a recreation room with the inclusion of a pool table that greatly expands the living space of this home. It also creates the sense of courtyard intimacy in both the front entryway, welcoming visitors through a covered porch, as well as the back, through a bank of tall casement windows that overlooks a backyard packed with patio and water. A visitor can turn one way or the other, and in either case, find themselves in a beautiful common room that adjoins to the great room of the main house.

The back of the home is all about recreation. Windows and patio glass doors of the main home overlook the pool area, while the recreation pool table and breezeway room, with its tall bank of casement windows, borders the patio area on the other side.

The great room has a sunny, open feeling, overlooked by a loft and staggered windows.

A great room is an enchanting, sun-filled room that overlooks the pool area.

Blue and white furnishings add to the open, beach-y feel of this bright home. The kitchen and dining area are part of the open great room that fills the back of the main house.

The master suite on the first floor enjoys a private wing of the home, while upstairs a guestroom and study create additional living space.

Aqua Gem

Manufactured by
Rocky Mountain Log Homes

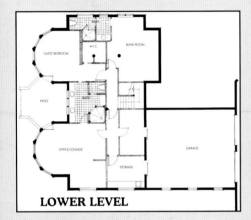

LOWER LEVEL

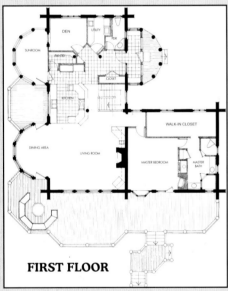

FIRST FLOOR

Angles and multi-faceted sides add interest to this pretty pond-side abode, creating a new twist on the age-old art of the log-home.

A pretty log cabin adds peaks and promontories to a pond-side view. Semi-circular log-trimmed bump-outs extend the view from inside, and infuse this comfortable home with sunshine. A lower level offers parking, an office/lounge area, and guest accommodations, while the main floor accounts for the bulk of the living space along with a master bedroom with a to-die-for walk-in closet. A wealth of angles add interest to the home, as every angle incorporates surprises, each illuminated by a generous allowance of picture window.

A central fireplace adds radiant heat to both living room and master bedroom.

Far left:
A sunroom provides an indoor garden where the homeowners love to dine and relax.

Left:
Another semi-circular bump-out has been furnished for semi-formal dining.

The master-suite has been finished in traditional log style, complete with chinking. A cathedral roof and big gable windows, as well as a glassed-in corner shower, are new additions to this traditional architecture.

Familial Embrace

Photography by David Bailey
Manufactured by Southland Log Homes
Built by Albert Phillips
*Designed by Southland Log Homes
Design Group*

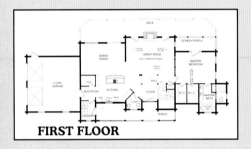

FIRST FLOOR

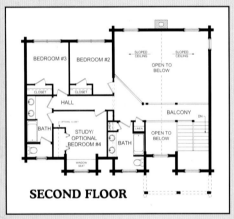

SECOND FLOOR

Top:
Southern yellow pine logs clad this handsome family home, approached via garage by the family, or via a sheltered doorway by guests.

Bottom:
The scale of the great room is emphasized in great stretches of southern yellow pine logs that span the breadth and height of the open room.

A wonderful covered porch provides welcome to a home designed with family in mind. The family most often enters through the garage, with a mudroom, pantry, and laundry providing a practical passage to the kitchen and family rooms beyond. The children share a bath upstairs, along with a study and private recreation room. Downstairs, the parents have their own wing of the house with a master suite accessed near the stairwell, and a private, screen porch.

A balcony overlooks the great room.

Below and following page: Kitchen and dining areas are part of the expansive, open, central portion of the home.

The master suite sits under its own roof, creating a cathedral ceiling for this generous space.

Opposite page:
A balcony overlooks the great room and provides passage to bedrooms on one side of the house.

Left:
A window seat is one of the draws of a study room upstairs.

Upstairs, the children enjoy their own bedrooms, and a bath and study to share.

Packing It In

Photography by Bill Kund
Manufactured by
Stonemill Log Homes, Inc.
Built by Stonemill Log Homes, Inc.
Designed by Stonemill Log Homes, Inc./
Quinn Pillsworth

FIRST FLOOR

SECOND FLOOR

Above:
From the front, this home looks like it came right out of the 17th century. Flanked by chimneys, with chinked logs and a shedrow porch roof, it could easily have housed one of our forefathers.

Below:
A sunroom and porch roof adds outdoor living to the back of this beautiful log home.

From the front, this home looks like a traditional, historic log cabin. Inside, it's been organized much like the traditional American colonial home, with rooms radiating off a central entry hall, and upstairs bedrooms accessed via a central staircase. It differs drastically, however, in scale. The living room rises all the way to the roof, creating gathering areas our forefather's never dreamed of for their homes.

Far left:
A stretch of front porch embodies the American dream, with rocking chairs and architecture that will survive for future ancestors.

Left:
The great room is an inspiring place, overlooked by massive beams, and made cozy by chinked logs.

Above, left:
A fireplace warms the dining area, furnished with comfortable, upholstered chairs that encourage diners to linger. It is one of three fireplaces working in the home.

Above, right:
Country aesthetics predominate in the kitchen, a central hub that connects to the great room, dining areas, and a utility room.

The master bedroom is furnished with chinked log walls, like those found throughout the house.

Suite Deal

Photography by Image Studios
Manufactured by
Strongwood Log Home Company
Built by Strongwood Construction
Designed by
Strongwood Log Home Company

FIRST FLOOR

SECOND FLOOR

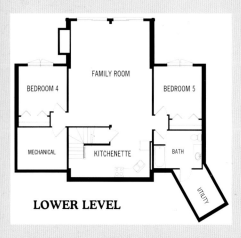

LOWER LEVEL

This stunning home made the most of every view, featuring three stories of floor-to-ceiling windows. Within, beautiful details have been lovingly bestowed on this home, from wood balusters and a wood-paneled ceiling in the great room, to the lighting fixtures and other furnishings that add character and elegance to this home. This intelligent design also includes a finished lower level that opens to a wonderful patio outfitted with a hot tub.

The inviting and rustic front entrance sets the stage for the many welcoming aspects of this home. In the back, an expansive deck is accessible from both the kitchen and screen porch. The master suite has its own cozy, private deck overlooking the hot tub and patio off the finished lower level.

Opposite page and left:
The centrally located great room is open to both the kitchen and dining areas, with a focus on the stone fireplace.

A view from the balcony illustrates how the great room is laid out.

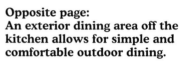

Opposite page:
An exterior dining area off the kitchen allows for simple and comfortable outdoor dining.

Granite countertop cuts a clean centerline through the kitchen, providing lots of work and dining space for the family.

Lake Luster

*Photography by
Tom Stewart Photography
Manufactured by Tennessee Log Homes
Built by Lonesome Dove Contractor
Designed by Mosscreek*

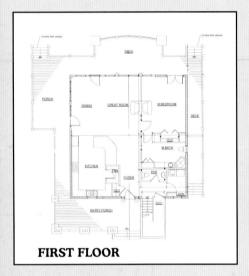

FIRST FLOOR

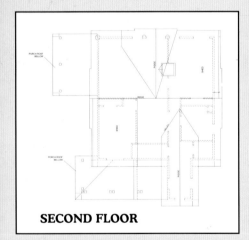

SECOND FLOOR

A lake-front lot dictated the design of the home: the wall of windows feeds the view to the great room beyond. A second-floor balcony creates a private viewing post for an upstairs bedroom.

A central great room and a wall of windows overlooking a lake are the focus of this house design. The big central area is jealously guarded from encroachment, with the bulk of the first floor enjoying the view, even from the kitchen against the far wall of the great room. The master suite downstairs opens to the back deck, while two smaller bedrooms feed off a loft area where the same view can be enjoyed bird's-eye style. Porch and decking surround the entire home, moving a lot of the living out of doors.

Left and above:
A view was carefully cultivated in a
great room wall that stacks windows
and sliding glass doors to maximize
glimpses of the lake beyond.

A balcony-rail adds architecture to
the lofty overlook.

Red cabinetry makes a contemporary statement in this home that mixes traditional with the efficiency of modern appliances.

Separate but Equal

Photography by Roger Wade Studios
Manufactured by
Town & Country Cedar Homes

FIRST FLOOR

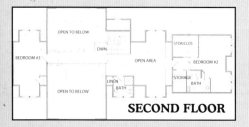

SECOND FLOOR

A pretty stone pathway invites visitors to approach this spacious home.

Signature dormers, customized peak trimwork, and fieldstone adorn all sides of this northern white cedar home.

A custom crafted front door personalizes the home's entrance.

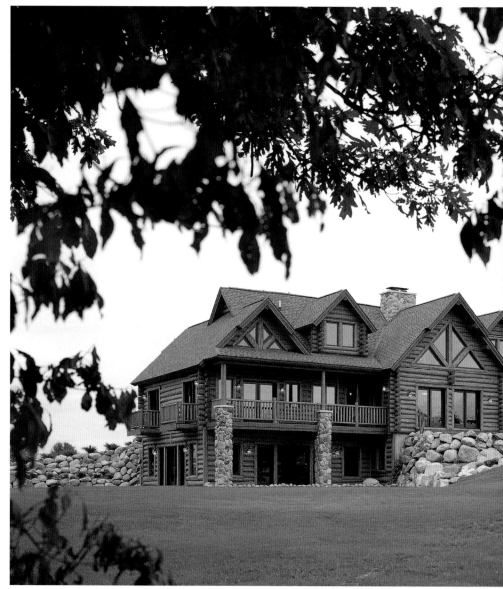

The great room is inspiring, exposing the interior of a complicated roofline. A balcony traverses the central chimney and adjoins the upper level guest suites with a loft library.

The kitchen is part of the passageway between the center of the home and the garage entry. A pantry across the hall creates extra storage so cabinetry is only needed on two walls.

Opposite page and left:
A formal dining area seats guests between the two-sided fireplace and a wall of glass.

The lofty master bedroom extends toward it's own wall of glass and sports four private balconies, overlooking a lush expanse of open green.

All Decked Out

Photography by
Franklin and Esther Schmidt
Manufactured by
Ward Cedar Log Homes
Built by Gabe Shank Builders
Designed by Ward Cedar Log Homes

FIRST FLOOR

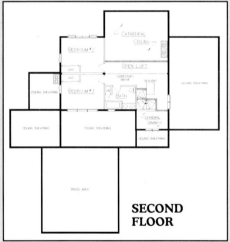

SECOND FLOOR

Top:
A modest approach belies the open spaces and bright rooms to be found beyond.

Bottom:
Two rows of windows feed light to the interior and add contemporary flair to this log structure.

A log home takes on a contemporary façade in this innovative home. The front approach is modest, with a garage and small covered entryway to welcome visitors into a haven that opens up into the sunlight. Deck wraps the entire back of this home, creating a splendid skirt and an extension of the living spaces on the backside of this home.

**A circular stairwell in the entryway
adds a twist to the foyer.**

The kitchen and a dining nook share
a corner of windows and door opening to an elevated deck.

Diagonal boards illustrate the innovative applications explored in this contemporary log home.

Opposite page:
A loft area is dedicated to the children, with two bedrooms and a shared bath, as well as the appeal of a balcony that overlooks the sunken living room.

Contributors

The Log Homes Council
National Association of Home Builders
1201 15th Street, NW
Washington, DC 20005
800-368-5242
www.loghomes.org

Alta Log Homes
46966 State Hwy 30
Halcottsville, NY 12438
800-926-2582
www.altaloghomes.com

Barna Log Homes
22459 Alberta St.
Oneida, TN 37841
800-962-4734
www.barnahomes.com

Beaver Mountain Log & Cedar Homes
1740 County Highway 48
Deposit, NY 13754
888-857-2158
www.beavermtn.com

Custom Log Homes, Inc.
PO Box 218
Stevensville, MT 59870
406-777-5202
www.customlogs.com

Estemerwalt Log Homes
505 Adams Pond Rd.
Honesdale, PA 18431
800-515-2060
www.estemerwalt.com

Expedition Log Homes, LLC
PO Box 700080
Oostburg, WI 53070
877-250-3300
www.expeditionloghomes.com

Gastineau Log Homes, Inc.
10423 Old Hwy. 54
New Bloomfield, MO 65063
800-654-9253
www.oakloghome.com

Golden Eagle Log Homes
4421 Plover Road
Wisconsin Rapids, WI 54494
800-270-5025
www.goldeneagleloghomes.com

Hearthstone, Inc.
1630 E. Hwy. 25/70
Dandridge, TN 37725
800-247-4442
www.hearthstonehomes.com

Heritage Log Homes
One Heritage Place
Kodak, TN 37764
800-456-4663
www.heritagelog.com

Hiawatha Log Homes, Inc.
M28 East
Munising, MI 49862
906-387-4121
www.hiawatha.com

Hilltop Log & Timber Homes
P. O. Box 170, 88 Pond Road
Bowdoinham, ME 04008
207-666-8840 or 800-622-4608
www.hilltoploghomes.com

Hochstetler Milling, Ltd.
552 St. Rt. 95
Loudonville, OH 44842
800-368-1015

Honest Abe Log Homes
9995 Clay County Hwy
Moss, TN 38575
800-231-3695
www.honestabeloghomes.com

Kuhns Bros. Log Homes, Inc.
390 Swartz Road
Lewisburg, PA 17837
800-326-9614
www.kuhnsbros.com

Meadowlark Log Homes, Inc.
50 Meadowlark Lane, MT 59923
Libby, MT
800-850-8554
www.meadowlarklog.com

Meadow Valley Log Homes
800 McEvoy Street
Mauston, WI 53948
800-491-4423
www.mvloghomes.com

Northeastern Log Homes, Inc.
PO Box 46
Kenduskadg, ME 04450
800-624-2797
www.northeasternlog.com

Precision Craft Log & Timber Homes
711 E. Broadway Avenue
Meridian, ID 83642
800-729-1320
www.precisioncraft.com

Real Log Homes
PO Box 202
Hartland, BT 05048
802-436-2123
www.realloghomes.com

Rocky Mountain Log Homes
1883 Hwy. 93 South
Hamilton, VT 59840
406-363-5680
www.rmlh.com

Southland Log Homes, Inc.
PO Box 1668
Irmo, SC 29063
803-781-5100
www.southlandloghomes.com

Stonemill Log Homes
10024 Parkside Drive
Knoxville, TN 37922
800-438-8274
www.stonemill.com

Strongwood Log Homes, Co.
711Shadow Road
Waupaca, WI 54981
866-258-4818
www.strongwoodloghomes.com

Tennessee Log Homes, Inc.
2537 Decatur Pike
Athens, TN 37303
800-251-9218
www.tnloghomes.com

Town & Country Cedar Homes
4772 US 131 South
Petoskey, MI 49770
800-9683178
www.cedarhomes.com

Ward Cedar Log Homes
PO Box 72
Houlton, ME 04730
800-341-1566
www.wardcedarloghomes.com